All the Places to Go . . . How Will You Know?
Participant's Guide

Tyndale House Publishers, Inc.
Carol Stream, Illinois

JOHN ORTBERG

ALL THE

PLACES

TO GO

HOW WILL YOU KNOW?

God has placed before you
an open door.
What will you do?

Visit Tyndale online at www.tyndale.com.

TYNDALE and Tyndale's quill logo are registered trademarks of Tyndale House Publishers, Inc.

All the Places to Go . . . How Will You Know? Participant's Guide

Designed by Jacqueline L. Nuñez

Published in association with Yates & Yates (www.yates2.com).

ISBN 978-1-4964-0460-2

Printed in the United States of America

21   20   19   18   17
7   6

Contents

Introduction

THANK YOU FOR CHOOSING to discover the God of open doors and to learn how to respond to the options set before you. This discussion guide is designed to accompany the *All the Places to Go . . . How Will You Know?* video curriculum. Our hope is that you will use this guide in a group setting such as a Bible study, Sunday school class, or other small group gathering to work through the study.

Each group should have a leader who is responsible for starting the video, keeping track of time, and guiding discussion. The leader is also the person who may read questions aloud, prompt group members to respond, and ensure that everyone has the opportunity to participate.

This study is meant to complement the book *All the Places to Go . . . How Will You Know?*, written by John Ortberg. Group members are encouraged to have a copy of the book, although the study can be completed with just the participant's guide and the video.

We are excited that by participating in this study, your group will be ready to step out in faith and embrace all the extraordinary opportunities that await.

Materials Needed

IN ORDER TO GET THE MOST out of studying *All the Places to Go . . . How Will You Know?*, the following materials are suggested in addition to the participant's guide:

- *All the Places to Go . . . How Will You Know?* book (one per group member)
- Television or computer monitor
- DVD player
- Watch or clock for monitoring time
- Bible (one per group member)
- Pen or pencil for each participant

Leader Tips

THE FOLLOWING ARE TIPS that will help you lead a successful *All the Places to Go . . . How Will You Know?* study.

- The study works equally well in both church and home group settings.
- Preview the part you will be studying on the DVD, and familiarize yourself with the video teaching notes, the discussion questions, and the Bible study prompts before your group time begins.
- Gather the necessary materials for each session before your group time begins.
- You may not have time to discuss all the questions during your group time—that's okay! Choose those that best fit your group, and encourage everyone to participate.
- Make sure to read "A Word to Leaders" on page xiii prior to starting your study. This is written to help you reflect on the main theme of the study and to consider your own hopes and desires for the group you're about to lead.
- Please read "A Word to Participants" with your group before starting your study time together. This section will help your group prepare for the study together.

- Before closing your group time, be sure to encourage
  participants to dig deeper into the lesson by completing
  the suggested activities given at the end of each session.

A Word to Leaders

THANK YOU FOR YOUR WILLINGNESS to lead a group through this study of *All the Places to Go . . . How Will You Know?* As your group begins, remember that you are a leader because God has put a desire in your heart to help people gain the full measure of understanding what it means to follow Jesus.

Our prayer is that God will use this video curriculum to open the eyes of the people in your group to the numerous opportunities God gives them each day and that, by stepping through the open doors, you and your group will grow closer to him.

A Word to Participants

OPEN DOORS MAY EXCITE YOU—or terrify you. Whatever your response is, you will approach many open doors throughout your life. What will you do?

As you study *All the Places to Go . . . How Will You Know?* our prayer is that you will learn to recognize open doors and trust the God who gave them to you as you walk through.

THE OPEN DOOR

Every morning is an open door; every moment can become one. Some of us see the doors and seize them, and so life becomes a divine adventure. Some of us shrink back or fail to see. A room with no door is a prison. To fail to embrace the open door is to miss the work God has made for us to do. If we want to experience more of the Spirit of God in our lives, we need to train ourselves to look for and respond to moments of divine opportunity.

ALL THE PLACES TO GO, CHAPTER 1

VIDEO TEACHING NOTES

As you watch the video, use the space below to take notes. Some key points and quotes are provided here as reminders.

David's Story

Frustrated by a lack of opportunities in global health, David created an opportunity, starting a clinic in Mexico to provide basic health screenings for poor people.

Teaching 1: John Ortberg

What can a door mean? What does it mean when it's open? What does it mean when *God* has opened it?

How can you recognize divine opportunities?

Open doors are not necessarily . . .

- thrilling.
- pleasant, smooth experiences.
- free of hardship and struggle.
- a guarantee.
- a set of detailed instructions.
- easy to choose.

QUOTABLE: "God doesn't say, 'I've set before you a hammock.'"

An open door is an opportunity provided by God, to act *with* God and *for* God.

The example of Abram leaving his home in Ur (Genesis 12).

QUOTABLE: "To find out what's on the other side of an open door, you'll have to go through."

Ally's Story

After winning the American Gladiator competition, Ally used her fame to set up fitness camps. While her organization is not exactly a Christian ministry, its Christian leaders have found numerous opportunities to share God's love and truth.

Teaching 2: John Ortberg

Characteristics of people with a "closed-door mind-set":

- believe there is only a fixed amount of talent in the world
- try to assure success in life
- don't risk failure

Characteristics of people with an "open-door mind-set":

- ready to embrace the challenge
- unhindered by uncertainty
- understand that they are blessed in order to bless

VIDEO GROUP DISCUSSION

1. What did you learn from the examples of David and Ally? What open doors did they encounter, and how did they respond? You may not be a med student or a fitness champ, but what divine opportunities might come your way?

2. We encounter various opportunities every day. How do you know whether God has opened a particular door or whether it's just your own ambition, the nudging of a meddling relative, or sheer coincidence?

3. God's call for Abram to leave Ur and go to Canaan was a divinely opened door. What divinely opened doors have you experienced in your life? How have you responded?

4. How would you describe the difference between the closed-door mind-set and the open-door mind-set? Do you know people who exemplify one kind or the other?

On the continuum below, where would you put your own mind-set? Put an X at that spot.

⟵┼┼┼┼┼┼┼┼┼┼┼┼┼┼┼┼┼┼┼┼┼┼┼┼┼┼┼┼┼┼┼┼┼┼┼┼┼┼⟶

VERY CLOSED   *VERY OPEN*

Where do you think you were, say, ten years ago? Put an O at that spot, and then draw an arrow from the O to the X. What's your trend? Are you opening or closing?

5. A divine opportunity is never just for your own benefit, John Ortberg said. We are blessed in order to bless others. In the video, Ally was a good example of this, using her temporary fame to create a camp program that would help others both physically and spiritually. Have you seen this sort of thing happen in your world? Do you know people who have seized opportunities to help others?

As you think about the possibilities in your own life, is there a particular group of people you would like to bless—or a particular way you might bless others?

GROUP BIBLE EXPLORATION

1. Read together Revelation 3:8:

   I know your deeds. See, I have placed before you an open door that no one can shut. I know that you have little strength, yet you have kept my word and have not denied my name.

   This passage was written to Christians in a town of Asia Minor (modern Turkey) known as Philadelphia. The context indicates that they were facing persecution. What else can we surmise about these believers from just this verse?

Why would it be important for God to tell them that "no one can shut" the door he opens? How would that make them feel?

Do you think our deeds have anything to do with the open doors God sets before us? Why or why not?

2. Read together Genesis 12:1-3:

The LORD had said to Abram, "Go from your country, your people and your father's household to the land I will show you.

"I will make you into a great nation,
*   and I will bless you;*
I will make your name great,
*   and you will be a blessing.*
I will bless those who bless you,
*   and whoever curses you I will curse;*
and all peoples on earth
*   will be blessed through you."*

Where was Abram leaving *from*? Where was he going *to*?

How do you think he felt about this calling? Excited? Scared? Flattered? Challenged?

Five times in these verses we find the word *bless* in some form. Who is doing the blessing, and who is getting blessed?

What do you think this "blessing" means? It's clearly more than good wishes after a sneeze. *How* will people be blessed?

3. Read together Genesis 12:4-6:

   So Abram went, as the LORD had told him; and Lot went with him. Abram was seventy-five years old when he set out from Harran. He took his wife Sarai, his nephew Lot, all the possessions they had accumulated and the people they had

*acquired in Harran, and they set out for the land of Canaan,
and they arrived there. Abram traveled through the land as far
as the site of the great tree of Moreh at Shechem. At that time
the Canaanites were in the land.*

How did Abram respond to God's calling? How do you think
his wife felt about this?

Apparently this was a two-step migration. It seems that Abram
got his father, Terah, to uproot the whole family and go as far as
the city of Harran (see Genesis 11:31). On the Fertile Crescent,
curving from the Persian Gulf to Canaan, Harran is about
halfway between these locations. What hints do we get in verses
4-6 about what their life was like at this halfway point?

While he was still in Harran, do you think Abram had gone
through that "open door" yet? As we seek to follow God's call,
do halfway measures help us to get there or distract us from
following through?

This passage ends with the news that "Canaanites were in the land." What would this mean for Abram and his family? What sort of "Canaanites" might be on the other side of the open doors God sets before us?

4. Read together Numbers 13:1-2, 27-28 (NLT):

The LORD now said to Moses, "Send out men to explore the land of Canaan, the land I am giving to the Israelites. Send one leader from each of the twelve ancestral tribes." . . .

This was their report to Moses: "We entered the land you sent us to explore, and it is indeed a bountiful country—a land flowing with milk and honey. Here is the kind of fruit it produces. But the people living there are powerful, and their towns are large and fortified. We even saw giants there, the descendants of Anak!"

In this case the "open door" also leads to Canaan, but it's centuries after Abraham. After years of slavery in Egypt, Moses is leading the Israelites through the wilderness, *back* to their Promised Land. How does *God* describe Canaan in verse 2?

How did the twelve leaders describe Canaan?

How do you think they felt about seizing this divine opportunity?

5. Read together what Joshua and Caleb said in Numbers 14:7-10 (NLT).

"The land we traveled through and explored is a wonderful land! And if the LORD is pleased with us, he will bring us safely into that land and give it to us. It is a rich land flowing with milk and honey. . . . Don't be afraid of the people of the land. . . . The LORD is with us!"

Ten of the twelve leaders refused to enter this giant-infested land. Only two, Caleb and Joshua, wanted to move through that open door. Did Caleb and Joshua disagree with the facts presented in the majority report? Did they question the goodness of the land? Did they dispute that there were giants there? What was the one point on which they differed?

How can we bring the Caleb and Joshua Factor ("The Lord is with us!") into our lives as a regular tendency?

IN CLOSING

As you end the study today, pray together for openness. Open yourselves up to God's calling. Ask him for the courage to be open to his leading—no matter how many "giants" you'll have to face.

Before session 2, complete the "On Your Own between Sessions" section. You might want to start the next session by asking other members of your group to share what they learned from these exercises.

ON YOUR OWN BETWEEN SESSIONS

1. In the story we studied from Numbers 13–14, there were twelve leader/scouts, and they voted 10 to 2 *against* seizing the opportunity God was giving them. Now let's imagine that you have twelve voices in your head. This is not a referendum on your sanity, but we all have ways of thinking through the issues we face. When you have an open door before you, do you race to go through it without a second thought? Then your vote is 12 to 0 *for*. If for every positive reason you generally think of eleven reasons *not* to do something, then maybe you're 11 to 1 *against*. Or maybe you're right in the middle, yes or no, 6 to 6. On the chart below, draw a line dividing the yeas and nays, indicating what your general tendency is when confronted with a divine opportunity.

SEIZING THE OPPORTUNITY

1	2	3	4	5	6	7	8	9	10	11	12

The truth is, there's often value in being careful, but once we know the Lord has opened a door, we need to open ourselves to those possibilities. If your natural tendency is to "go for it," great, but you might seek to cultivate wisdom about what you "go for" (and our next session will help with that). If you're generally closed to new opportunities, even if they're coming from God, then openness will be something to work on.

2. Read the story of David and Goliath in 1 Samuel 17. If you're used to a particular translation, mix it up a bit by going with a new one, just to get fresh eyes on the story. This is a familiar tale—you know what happens—but let's pay special attention to the open mind-set and the closed mind-set. Who is open in this story and who is closed? What details support this?

WHO?	OPEN OR CLOSED?	EVIDENCE
DAVID'S BROTHERS		
SAUL		
ISRAELITE ARMY		
DAVID		

The scouts who explored Canaan were right: there were giants in the land, like Goliath. But David took him on, armed with the same attitude that propelled Caleb and Joshua—the Lord is with us (see 1 Samuel 17:37).

How can that attitude help you confront the "giants" in your life?

3. Read the story of the rich young ruler in Luke 18:18-30, but first put aside any assumptions or defenses. Imagine yourself as the rich young ruler's personal assistant, watching this story

unfold. What do you see and hear? How does this make you feel?

What "open door" was set before the man? What did he do about it? Why? Let's consider his reasoning. Putting yourself in the rich young ruler's place, fill out the following chart as best you can.

REASONS TO DO WHAT JESUS SAID	REASONS NOT TO DO WHAT JESUS SAID

Do any of those reasons, on either side, come into play as you're considering some (possibly) divine opportunity? How do you weigh those reasons?

4. Life Experiment: Open Day. Pick a day this week to experiment with openness. Shortly after you wake up, talk with God. Indicate your desire to be open to whatever he brings your way that day—whatever that means. Then, as you go through the day—breakfast, commute, work, lunch, family time, a trip to the corner store, hanging with friends, etc.—keep this in mind. You're being *open*. You don't need to plan to do anything religious. Just be open to what God brings.

   This might mean paying attention to the people around you. What needs do they have? How can you show them the love of Christ? It might mean taking some extra time with a friend or a family member who needs to talk. It might mean enjoying a sunset or a great piece of music. Or God might throw a challenge your way. Will you face it openly, trusting in his help?

5. Life Experiment: Follow-Up. After trying the Open Day experiment, talk about it with someone else. Was it good, weird, hard, instructive, life changing, pointless, etc.?

   Consider talking about it when you gather for the next session of *All the Places to Go*.

RECOMMENDED READING

In preparation for session 2, you may want to read chapter 5 of *All the Places to Go . . . How Will You Know?* by John Ortberg. To review the material from session 1, read chapters 1–2.

DOOR #1 OR DOOR #2?

Choosing comes from the core of who we are. When we truly choose, we have no one to blame and nowhere to hide. Choosing thrills us. Choosing scares us. Choosing is central to personhood. . . . God wants us to learn to choose well.

ALL THE PLACES TO GO, CHAPTER 5

VIDEO TEACHING NOTES

As you watch the video, use the space below to take notes. Some key points and quotes are provided here as reminders.

Kevin's Story

Kevin planned to become a doctor to provide for his poor mother, but God led him into ministry—and then even further, from his comfortable church job to a low-paying ministry in a difficult area.

Teaching 1: John Ortberg

Making decisions is stressful.

We say we want to know God's will (like King Saul), but do we really?

QUOTABLE: "God wants us to be excellent choosers."

Choosing doors involves a process:

- recognize opportunity
- identify options
- evaluate
- choose
- learn

Decision making involves wisdom, which God wants us to ask for (see James 1:5).

QUOTABLE: "God's primary will for your life is not the achievements you accrue. It's the person you become."

Amanda's Story

After being injured in the Boston Marathon blast, Amanda began to think more deeply about her purpose and her passion. Using her marketing background, she started a new company that provides opportunities for struggling artisans in the developing world.

Teaching 2: John Ortberg

People with small souls have small problems.

People who live with largeness of soul are occupied by large problems.

You need a God-sized problem.

Very often, purpose comes when people begin to pay attention to what moves their hearts. What is breaking your heart?

Get wise people around you and listen to them.

Avoid restricted thinking. God may have more options than you know.

Wise discernment does not guarantee success.

Wisdom is a person—Jesus.

VIDEO GROUP DISCUSSION

1. In Kevin's story, we saw a man reworking his financial goals as he tried to follow God's direction. How important are economic factors in the life decisions you make? How important do you think they should be? (And please, don't just give the spiritual-sounding answer here. If you got a job offer for twice the money you're making now, how appealing would that be?)

2. John Ortberg suggested "practicing" our decision-making skills on the minor choices of life so we'll be ready to make the big decisions wisely. Does this make sense to you? Have you ever tried it? If so, what have you learned? Is there a specific small decision that has taught you something about making larger decisions? How?

3. The video laid out a decision-making process: recognize opportunity, identify options, evaluate, choose, and learn. Let's see how that works in our everyday lives.

   Take a moment right now to think about a *minor* decision that you need to make in the next few days. It might be as simple as where to go or what to have for dinner, or what TV show to watch, or what to do after work tomorrow. Note: These are intentionally small decisions, and this process may seem like much ado about nothing, but it's a test case. Let's see if we can learn something about decision making.

   Recognize opportunity: Is this a chance to relax, communicate, learn something, exercise, try a new experience, invest in something valuable, etc.?

   Identify options: What are the two or three top possibilities here? List them on the left side of the chart below.

OPTIONS	EVALUATION (good or bad)
....	....
....	....
....	....

   Evaluate: On the right side of the chart, write some thoughts about what's good or bad about these options, as well as other factors that might be neutral.

Choose: Based on your evaluation, which seems like the best choice?

Learn: We can learn now about the process of decision making, but a lot of our learning won't come until we see how these choices play out.

Now that you've gone through this thought track on your own, could you share your process with the whole group? Don't worry if it seems trivial. That's the point!

Do you think this process would be more effective or less effective if you used it with a major decision, like a job change, a move, or a big purchase?

4. How did the hardships of life affect the decisions made by Kevin and Amanda, whom we met in this session?

Do you think tough circumstances usually bring about good decisions or bad decisions?

Here's what Amanda said: "I think, more than anything, it was this instant at the marathon, this flash, that really reconnected me with who I am deep down, the person I've always been, and I had just put that on hold for a couple of decades. But it reminded me instantly of who I am and what I care about and galvanized me into action."

Have you seen that with other people, or perhaps in your life—a crisis "galvanizing" you and bringing about a key decision? What happened?

5. "People with small souls have small problems," John Ortberg said. What did he mean by that? Do you agree?

If that's true, what can we do to get "larger souls"?

GROUP BIBLE EXPLORATION

1. Read together Philippians 1:9-11:

   This is my prayer: that your love may abound more and more in knowledge and depth of insight, so that you may be able to discern what is best and may be pure and blameless for the day of Christ, filled with the fruit of righteousness that comes through Jesus Christ—to the glory and praise of God.

   In your own words, what is Paul praying for?

   What does he mean by the words *insight* and *discern*?

   Let's connect these concepts to the rest of the passage. First, how do insight and discernment connect with *love*?

Second, how do insight and discernment help us produce the "fruit of righteousness"?

2. Read together James 1:2-5.

Consider it pure joy, my brothers and sisters, whenever you face trials of many kinds, because you know that the testing of your faith produces perseverance. Let perseverance finish its work so that you may be mature and complete, not lacking anything. If any of you lacks wisdom, you should ask God, who gives generously to all without finding fault, and it will be given to you.

Can you trace a connection from trials to perseverance to maturity to wisdom? How?

In the video, John Ortberg said, "Discerning open doors is never the same as finding guaranteed success. God actually called many people to walk through doors that would lead to enormous difficulty and not external reward." How does this passage from James 1 support that idea?

Have you ever asked God for wisdom? What happened?

3. Read together the following sections from Proverbs 8:

Does not wisdom call out?
  Does not understanding raise her voice? (verse 1)

Listen, for I have trustworthy things to say;
  I open my lips to speak what is right.
My mouth speaks what is true,
  for my lips detest wickedness.
All the words of my mouth are just;
  none of them is crooked or perverse.
To the discerning all of them are right;
  they are upright to those who have found knowledge.
Choose my instruction instead of silver,
  knowledge rather than choice gold,
for wisdom is more precious than rubies,
  and nothing you desire can compare with her. (verses 6-11)

I love those who love me,
  and those who seek me find me. (verse 17)

Blessed are those who listen to me,
  watching daily at my doors,
  waiting at my doorway.
For those who find me find life
  and receive favor from the LORD.
But those who fail to find me harm themselves;
  all who hate me love death. (verses 34-36)

Does anything in this text surprise you? Does it give you a new perspective on wisdom?

How valuable is wisdom? What are its "perks"?

In what ways does wisdom "love" those who love wisdom?

The mention of doors, gates, and streets in this chapter suggests that wisdom should be a part of our daily, walking-around life. So, what's the wisest thing you've done in the last day or so? (Or was there an everyday situation in which you should have asked for wisdom and didn't?)

4. The video referred to the story of Paul and Silas in the Philippian jail. Let's read that together from Acts 16:25-32:

About midnight Paul and Silas were praying and singing hymns to God, and the other prisoners were listening to them. Suddenly there was such a violent earthquake that the foundations of the prison were shaken. At once all the prison doors flew open, and everyone's chains came loose. The jailer woke up, and when he saw the prison doors open, he drew his sword and was about to kill himself because he thought the prisoners had escaped. But Paul shouted, "Don't harm yourself! We are all here!"

The jailer called for lights, rushed in and fell trembling before Paul and Silas. He then brought them out and asked, "Sirs, what must I do to be saved?"

They replied, "Believe in the Lord Jesus, and you will be saved—you and your household." Then they spoke the word of the Lord to him and to all the others in his house.

Do you think Paul and Silas might have been praying for release from prison? Why or why not?

So imagine that you're locked up with Paul and Silas. You're praying and singing hymns. Then . . . earthquake, chains loosen, doors open . . . what is the will of God for you in that moment? Walking out to freedom? Helping the other prisoners escape?

Here's what John Ortberg said about that: "Despite the door of his cell being wide open, [Paul] sees another, greater door opening to him. He has great clarity on the purpose of his life—to open spiritual doors for others."

Could you ever face a situation in which the obvious best choice—better job, better neighborhood, greater security, etc.—might actually take second place to a greater purpose . . . such as "opening spiritual doors for others"? *Have* you faced a situation like that?

5. Read together the quotation below from John 10:7-10 (ESV):

I am the door of the sheep. . . . If anyone enters by me, he will be saved and will go in and out and find pasture. The thief comes only to steal and kill and destroy. I came that they may have life and have it abundantly.

When Jesus said this, he was probably referring to a practice in which a shepherd would sit at the entry to a sheep pen. It's a beautiful image. So when he talks about the sheep "finding pasture," what is he talking about? How do *we*, as his flock, "find pasture"?

When he talks about having life "abundantly," is he talking about a heavenly existence, our life here and now, or both?

As we talk about the "open doors" in our lives, we're concerned about making the right choices. So if you're choosing between Door #1 and Door #2, how does it change your perspective to hear that Jesus himself is "the door"?

IN CLOSING

As you end the study today, pray together for wisdom. Perhaps some in the group want to share their personal dilemmas—what choices are weighing on them? Ask God for insight, for discernment, and for a daily ordering of priorities.

Before session 3, complete the "On Your Own between Sessions" section. You might want to review that section at the beginning of session 3.

ON YOUR OWN BETWEEN SESSIONS

1. The video mentioned the biblical story of King Saul and how he seemed to specialize in choosing the *wrong* doors. This is worth some personal study, especially in two important passages. First, read 1 Samuel 13:7-14.

   To go into battle or not? That was Saul's quandary. What reasons might he have considered on either side of that debate?

   Samuel was a prophet and priest, the spiritual leader of Israel. What do you think he had told Saul previously? In light of that, what, exactly, did Saul do wrong?

   Why do you think Saul considered it so important to offer the sacrifices?

   Second, look at a passage from a few chapters later, 1 Samuel 28:4-19.

   Saul had another, similar quandary. How did he try to get an answer? (Note: Urim was a stone on the high priest's breastplate that was sometimes interpreted to reveal God's will.)

How would you describe Saul's state of mind in verse 15?

Why do you think the Lord wasn't answering Saul?

This lesson is presenting an important idea that Saul had no clue about—and many people are just as clueless about today. "The will of God for your life" is not some impersonal force that you can interpret and manipulate through superstitions, rituals, lucky charms, or séances. Saul tried all of that and missed out on the personal relationship God wanted to have with him. When Jesus says, "I am the door," he is inviting us to choose a loving relationship with him, without manipulation—an abundant life in which we can find rich pasture. Regardless of what job or ministry we end up in, God's will for us is to know Jesus.

How can you choose a loving relationship with Jesus rather than superstition and manipulation?

2. Read Acts 13:1-3. Here we see the early church at work—leaders convening and deciding how to follow the Lord's leading. Let's see what we can learn about making group decisions.

Who was in the room? What are we told about them, and what can we guess?

What were they doing before the Spirit's instruction came to them?

How do you think the Spirit "said" this to them?

What did they do after the Spirit spoke to them? Why?

What are some tips we can gather here for modern churches, Christian ministries, or even small groups?

3. John Ortberg said in the video, "If you're not sure which door to choose, get around people whose character you trust, who have good judgment, who love you, and who care about your well-being. Very often God speaks wisdom into us through somebody else. Ask them, 'Could you speak wisdom into my life? Here's what I'm thinking. How does it sound to you?' Almost all train-wreck decisions people make (and we all make them) could be prevented just by asking one wise person to speak seriously into our lives . . . and then listening."

Who are your go-to people, friends who can help you discern what God wants?

Take some time now to think and pray . . . and jot down the names of three to five people who could help you. If you're married, make your spouse an *ex officio* member of this team. But are there three to five others? It might help to consider different areas of specialty.

Who can help you best with spiritual questions or crises?

Who can help you best with job issues or ministry questions?

Who can help you make wise choices regarding money, investments, giving, and purchases?

Who can help you best with relationship issues?

Who can tell you the truth even when it's hard to hear?

Who knows you best? Who is the world expert on YOU? Who listens when you talk? When you walk away from a conversation with them, you say, "They really *get* me."

Pray about which names you should put on this list. And pray for them, that God might even now be preparing them to speak wisdom into your life when you need it most.

4. On your own, or with your spouse or a close friend, think through past decisions you've made and do some analysis. What factors led to that particular decision? What can you learn about the decision-making process from that experience? Use the chart below, if it helps.

DECISION	FACTORS	LEARNING
BEST DECISIONS		
HARDEST DECISIONS		
WORST DECISIONS		

As you look back over the chart, can you assemble any words of wisdom to keep in mind for future decisions?

5. Life Experiment: Minor Choices.

Recognize your opportunities, and list three minor things you would normally do routinely in the coming week. Rethink those choices. It could be the way you commute to work or the coffee you order at the corner store or the shoes you wear or the TV show you watch. Pick three specific activities and go through the process mentioned in the video.

-
-
-

Identify what other options you have in each of these instances.

Evaluate pro and con factors.

You don't need to make a big spiritual issue out of these things, but know that God goes with you through life. Is there a particular option that he would prefer, or is he just happy to go along on this ride with you?

Choose what you will do when that opportunity comes along this week.

- You could choose to do what you always do—but now you know why.
- You could choose to adapt it in some way.
- You could choose to do something entirely different.

Learn. After you've done all three activities, consider what you've learned. Will you go back to the routine or keep trying something new?

RECOMMENDED READING

In preparation for session 3, you may want to read chapter 6 of *All the Places to Go . . . How Will You Know?*

HOW TO CROSS A THRESHOLD

I am not in charge of which doors will be presented to me through my life. I may not be able to force a closed door to open. I am not in charge of what's behind the door. But I am in charge of one dynamic: when a door is opened, I get to choose how I will respond. Sometimes it's what you do after the door opens that makes all the difference.

ALL THE PLACES TO GO, CHAPTER 6

VIDEO TEACHING NOTES

As you watch the video, use the space below to take notes. Some key points and quotes are provided here as reminders.

Linda's Story

In her job as a city bus driver, Linda has gained a reputation for her joyful and caring attitude. It's all because of Jesus.

Teaching 1: John Ortberg

What matters most is not *which* door we go through, but *how* we go through it.

QUOTABLE: "It's better to go through the wrong door with your best self than the best door with your wrong self."

Buyer's remorse—second thoughts over the effort, responsibility, and commitment in going through an open door. (Example: Israelites, freed from Egypt, talking about going back.)

"I don't feel peace about it." That's a trap. Internal anxiety. Emotional immaturity.

"Whatever you do, work *heartily*" (Colossians 3:23, emphasis added, ESV).

Heart = the core of the person. All of my energies.

Questions to ask in order to determine your level of commitment:

- Do I own the responsibility to grow? Do I read books and practice skills and meet with those further down the road to help me develop?
- Do I complain about difficulties in a way that can subtly rationalize a halfhearted involvement?
- Do I deal with discouragements by talking with God and asking for strength to persevere?

- Do I recognize and celebrate even small steps in the right direction?

Michael's Story

Michael used his carpentry skills to serve the poor in Jamaica. Even when the church discontinued those mission trips, he was committed to keep going there, at his own expense.

Teaching 2: John Ortberg

Three animal pictures used by Jesus for his disciples (see Matthew 10:16):

- Sheep among wolves
  - uninspiring
  - vulnerable
  - not heroic
- Wise as serpents
  - learning and awareness
  - self-aware
  - students of the world
- Innocent as doves
  - transformed character

VIDEO GROUP DISCUSSION

1. In the video, John Ortberg made some pretty strong state-
   ments—for instance, "It's better to go through the wrong
   door with your best self than the best door with your wrong
   self. Sometimes the way in which I go through a door matters
   more than which door I actually go through." Do you agree
   with this?

   If not, why not? If so, what are the implications of that in your
   life? Does this conviction lead to a more casual attitude about
   finding God's will, or does it keep you from fretting over the
   wisdom of past decisions as you wholeheartedly embrace your
   current challenges?

2. We saw the stories of Linda, a bus driver, and Michael, a
   carpenter. How would you describe their attitudes?

Did you especially connect with either one of them? Did they model an approach to life that you'd like to adopt? What would that look like in your context?

3. What did John Ortberg mean by "buyer's remorse"? How does it affect Christians who make big decisions about serving God?

Have you ever experienced this yourself? What happened?

4. In the video, John Ortberg made a big deal about people saying, "I just don't have peace about this." What was his point?

Do you agree with this saying? Do you think people sometimes use it as an excuse to keep from taking on a challenge? Have you ever done this?

Should we expect a sense of peace from God when we're deciding to do the right thing? Or is there a difference between the peace of avoiding challenges and the peace that comes from trusting God to help you through those challenges? How can you tell the difference between the two?

5. Toward the end of the video, John Ortberg mentioned three comparisons Jesus made with animals. We should be "sheep among wolves," "wise as serpents," and "innocent as doves." Which of those three *are* you, and which do you *need to be more like*? On the purely subjective scale below, mark where you see yourself in those three categories.

SHEEP AMONG WOLVES
(vulnerable but courageous, letting God use my weaknesses)
0 ------ 1 ------ 2 ------ 3 ------ 4 ------ 5 ------ 6 ------ 7 ------ 8 ------ 9 ------ 10

WISE AS SERPENTS
(aware of the world and my own place in it)
0 ------ 1 ------ 2 ------ 3 ------ 4 ------ 5 ------ 6 ------ 7 ------ 8 ------ 9 ------ 10

INNOCENT AS DOVES
(no false motives, forthright in sharing God's love)

0 ------ 1 ------ 2 ------ 3 ------ 4 ------ 5 ------ 6 ------ 7 ------ 8 ------ 9 ------ 10

GROUP BIBLE EXPLORATION

1. Read together Colossians 3:22-24:

   Slaves, obey your earthly masters in everything; and do it, not only when their eye is on you and to curry their favor, but with sincerity of heart and reverence for the Lord. Whatever you do, work at it with all your heart, as working for the Lord, not for human masters, since you know that you will receive an inheritance from the Lord as a reward. It is the Lord Christ you are serving.

   These verses come from a passage that gives instruction to husbands and wives, parents and children, slaves and masters. Why would it be important for Christian slaves to do their work "with all [their] heart" (verse 23)?

   You're not a slave, so how does this apply to you?

   In the video, John Ortberg emphasized the importance of living our lives *wholeheartedly*. He said the way we go through life is more important than which doors we choose. So if you find yourself "slaving away" in a less-than-ideal situation, does that mean you should choose a different door, or just work harder?

2. Read together Romans 12:9-16:

Love must be sincere. Hate what is evil; cling to what is good. Be devoted to one another in love. Honor one another above yourselves. Never be lacking in zeal, but keep your spiritual fervor, serving the Lord. Be joyful in hope, patient in affliction, faithful in prayer. Share with the Lord's people who are in need. Practice hospitality.

  Bless those who persecute you; bless and do not curse. Rejoice with those who rejoice; mourn with those who mourn. Live in harmony with one another. Do not be proud, but be willing to associate with people of low position. Do not be conceited.

At first glance, this seems like a to-do list of miscellaneous things Christians should do. How would you sum it up in one sentence?

In today's emphasis on wholeheartedness, we zeroed in on the words *zeal* and *fervor*. How does each of the items on this list describe a life of spiritual fervor, serving God with your whole heart?

3. If we're looking for something to tie all those commands together, it might be at the beginning of the same chapter. Read together Romans 12:1-2:

Therefore, I urge you, brothers and sisters, in view of God's mercy, to offer your bodies as a living sacrifice, holy and pleasing to God—this is your true and proper worship. Do not conform to the pattern of this world, but be transformed by the renewing of your mind. Then you will be able to test and approve what God's will is—his good, pleasing and perfect will.

How can someone be a "living sacrifice"? Clearly it's referring to the animals offered on the altar in ancient Israel—"holy and pleasing to God"—but those animals died. Does it make any sense to be a *living* sacrifice? How does that work?

What's the difference between *conforming* and being *transformed*?

This whole series has been dealing with the issue of God's will—focusing on the "doors" he leads us through. According to verse 2, how do we know what God wants for us? How does sacrificing ourselves and renewing our minds help us to test God's will?

4. Read together Matthew 10:16-20:

[Jesus said,] "I am sending you out like sheep among wolves. Therefore be as shrewd as snakes and as innocent as doves. Be on your guard; you will be handed over to the local councils and be flogged in the synagogues. On my account you will be brought before governors and kings as witnesses to them and to the Gentiles. But when they arrest you, do not worry about what to say or how to say it. At that time you will be given what to say, for it will not be you speaking, but the Spirit of your Father speaking through you."

As we learned in the video, Jesus used several animal illustrations with his disciples. But this was more than just a trip to the zoo. Jesus was sending his disciples out to serve him, and the comments that followed were actually prophetic. How does this context show us the behavior of being like sheep, serpents, and doves?

There is a built-in contradiction between being "shrewd as snakes" and "innocent as doves." Can we really be both? How does that work?

5. Read together 2 Samuel 6:14-16:

Wearing a linen ephod, David was dancing before the LORD with all his might, while he and all Israel were bringing up the ark of the LORD with shouts and the sound of trumpets.

As the ark of the LORD was entering the City of David, Michal daughter of Saul watched from a window. And when she saw King David leaping and dancing before the LORD, she despised him in her heart.

What was the occasion? Why was David so happy?

Do you know what an ephod is? (It's a sleeveless vest generally worn by priests.) Later the queen accused David of dancing "half-naked," so it was not a very modest garment. Why do you think David carried on like this in public? Didn't he realize that some people (like his wife) might be offended?

Have you ever done anything like this—erupting in praise and joy, regardless of what others think? If so, what happened?

Do you find that, in modern times, innocent acts of devotion are sometimes misunderstood by others? Is there anything we can, or should, do about that?

IN CLOSING

As you end the study today, take a moment to quiet down and get to the *heart* level. We're being challenged to serve God wholeheartedly, with zeal and a fervent spirit, with a "leaping and dancing" devotion. Determine to connect with God at your core and to commit what you can.

Pray together the opening words of Psalm 103: "Praise the LORD, my soul; *all my inmost being*, praise his holy name" (emphasis added).

Before session 4, complete the "On Your Own between Sessions" section. You might want to review that section at the beginning of session 4.

ON YOUR OWN BETWEEN SESSIONS

1. In the video, John Ortberg offered a series of questions to ask in order to gauge the wholeheartedness of a new endeavor. If you have recently "gone through an open door"—that is, seized a new opportunity to serve God—consider these questions:

   • Do I own the responsibility to grow? Do I read books and practice skills and meet with those further down the road to help me develop?
   • Do I complain about difficulties in a way that can subtly rationalize a halfhearted involvement?
   • Do I deal with discouragements by talking with God and asking for strength to persevere?
   • Do I recognize and celebrate even small steps in the right direction?

2. Do a personal study of Numbers 11. This is a classic example of "buyer's remorse"—the second-guessing we often do after starting a new commitment. In this case, the Israelites, recently freed from their slavery in Egypt, are complaining, and Moses has had enough.

   What emotions do you sense in the people, in Moses, and in the Lord?

How do you think you would have felt in this situation?

What does the Lord do for Moses and for the people?

Can you compare the Israelites' situation to an event from your own life? Have you ever complained as you began an exciting journey with God? What has he done to help you?

Don't miss the fact that the Lord has Moses gather a group of wise friends to "share the burden" (verse 17). Have you ever found that helpful? Who are the "elders" who help you?

3. Meditation: Sheep in the Midst of Wolves.

Take some quiet time this week to let your imagination roam: You're a sheep in Jesus' flock. There are dangers, but the Lord is your Shepherd. Let all those biblical references to sheep bounce through your mind (John 10, Luke 15, Isaiah 53, Psalm 23, etc.).

Then take it in a slightly different direction. One of the important things about sheep (as Jesus suggests in Matthew 10) is their vulnerability. They are weak, easily targeted, and wholly dependent on the shepherd.

Read Paul's riff on weakness from 2 Corinthians 12:9-10:

He said to me, "My grace is sufficient for you, for my power is made perfect in weakness." Therefore I will boast all the more gladly about my weaknesses, so that Christ's power may rest on me. That is why, for Christ's sake, I delight in weaknesses, in insults, in hardships, in persecutions, in difficulties. For when I am weak, then I am strong.

Let God speak that truth deep into your heart.

4. We're challenged to be "shrewd [or wise] as snakes" (Matthew 10:16). In the video, and even more so in the book *All the Places to Go*, John Ortberg defines that as *awareness*. We need to be aware of ourselves and how our unique abilities and traits interact with the world around us. This is what we saw in Linda the bus driver and Michael the carpenter. They knew what they had to offer (attitude, skills), and they offered it to the world.

On a scale of 0 to 10, how would you rate your self-awareness?

0 ------ 1 ------ 2 ------ 3 ------ 4 ------ 5 ------ 6 ------ 7 ------ 8 ------ 9 ------ 10

On a scale of 0 to 10, how would you rate your awareness of the world around you?

0 ------ 1 ------ 2 ------ 3 ------ 4 ------ 5 ------ 6 ------ 7 ------ 8 ------ 9 ------ 10

Using those two numbers, plot a point on this chart. Which quadrant are you in?

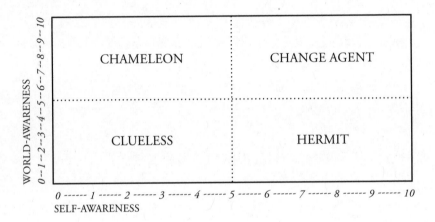

If you don't like where you are on that chart, what could you do to change it? How could you become more aware of yourself or of your world?

5. Life Experiment: Innocent as Doves. This week, do something kind or exuberant or meaningful, something that comes from the wholeness of your heart. Do this without regard to any naysayers. This is your "leaping and dancing" moment. It might be a gift you give, a song you sing, a call you make. It might be a random act of kindness you do for another person. You could rake your neighbor's leaves. Or pay the toll for the car behind you. Or give a gift card to the clerk at the convenience store. Or send an e-mail to a friend you've been taking for granted. You might plan this in advance, or you could wait for the Spirit to move you. Just be ready to move when he does.

RECOMMENDED READING

In preparation for session 4, you may want to read chapter 3 of *All the Places to Go* and skim over chapter 1 again.

THE DOORS WE OPEN FOR OTHERS

Every heart comes with a door. Having the door of someone's heart open to you is one of the great gifts of life. To respond well requires time, energy, vulnerability, and discernment.

ALL THE PLACES TO GO, CHAPTER 3

VIDEO TEACHING NOTES

As you watch the video, use the space below to take notes. Some key points and quotes are provided here as reminders.

Peter's Story

For Peter, an abusive childhood led to an addictive adulthood. But then God transformed his life. Now he seeks to employ those who need a second chance to live a productive life.

Teaching 1: John Ortberg

QUOTABLE: "Biblically speaking, open doors are divine invitations to make our lives count, with God's help, for the sake of others."

We live in a narcissistic culture (i.e., Facebook). We are "curators of our own selves."

FOMO: The Fear of Missing Out

We're afraid that other people are doing more interesting things than we're doing.

Wasn't FOMO behind the first sin? (See Genesis 3:1, 5.)

We have an insatiable hunger for more.

God can do "immeasurably more than all we ask or imagine" (Ephesians 3:20).

"What if?" people lead imaginative lives.

QUOTABLE: "Faith is, among other things, an act of the imagination."

Atlanta Story

A small group in Georgia helped refurbish the house of a family in their group, but then a flood washed it all away. They kept working, helping.

Teaching 2: John Ortberg

Ruth demonstrates remarkable commitment to others.

She "bet everything on love."

Ruth's devotion to Naomi resulted in open doors for both of them.

QUOTABLE: "Doors open when we really notice and care about people we might normally overlook."

We see our place in the world as God sees it.

VIDEO GROUP DISCUSSION

1. In the video, we met Peter, who was hiring others for his business. He said, "My job is to extend God's rule and reign, down here in this place, and that is what I live for." What does he mean by that? How can we extend God's Kingdom? Do you agree that this is something we should try to do? Do you feel you are doing this in your life? If so, how?

2. We also met the people of a small group who were rebuilding a house, and then rebuilding it again. How did you feel about that story? How would you have felt after the storm washed away all your hard work? Why do you think people would keep working so hard on that project?

   Have you ever been part of a group with that kind of passion for service? How has your group helped others?

3. John Ortberg used the term FOMO—Fear of Missing Out. Are you familiar with this idea? Have you experienced it in your life?

Do you think FOMO is a recent phenomenon, or just a new name for something that's always been around?

Do you think FOMO is a good thing or a bad thing—or neutral? Is there anything wrong with wanting the most out of life? What are some of the dangers that come with that?

4. "Love opens doors," said John Ortberg, and he showed us how this happened in the Bible with Ruth. Has it ever happened with you? Have you found that selfless actions have opened up new opportunities, new directions, or perhaps new relationships in your life? What are some examples?

5. In the video we were challenged to use our imaginations, to be "what if?" people. In your own words, how would you describe a "what if?" person?

Let's see if we can take a few minutes now to ask, "What if?" Think about some need that you're burdened about—not in your own life or your family, but in the larger church or community. Is there some issue—some problem—that God has laid on your heart? (See if you can name two to three issues of concern.)

Now *what if* we could do something about one of these needs? We have certain talents and resources that we could apply to these situations. For the moment, put aside all the naysaying. Turn off that voice in your head that says, "It'll never work. We can't do anything." We're using our imaginations. What crazy ideas could we come up with right now to show God's love in those dire situations?

GROUP BIBLE EXPLORATION

....

1. Read together Luke 12:13-21:

Someone in the crowd said to him, "Teacher, tell my brother to divide the inheritance with me."

Jesus replied, "Man, who appointed me a judge or an arbiter between you?" Then he said to them, "Watch out! Be on your guard against all kinds of greed; life does not consist in an abundance of possessions."

And he told them this parable: "The ground of a certain rich man yielded an abundant harvest. He thought to himself, 'What shall I do? I have no place to store my crops.' Then he said, 'This is what I'll do. I will tear down my barns and build bigger ones, and there I will store my surplus grain. And I'll say to myself, "You have plenty of grain laid up for many years. Take life easy; eat, drink and be merry."'

"But God said to him, 'You fool! This very night your life will be demanded from you. Then who will get what you have prepared for yourself?' This is how it will be with whoever stores up things for themselves but is not rich toward God."

Do you see any FOMO in this passage? Where? Was the original questioner afraid of missing out on his share of the inheritance? Was the rich fool afraid he would, at some point, not have enough grain?

Is FOMO just another term for greed, or is there more to it?

What does it mean to be "rich toward God"? How would that affect the rest of our lives?

2. Read together Ephesians 3:16-21:

I pray that out of his glorious riches he may strengthen you with power through his Spirit in your inner being, so that Christ may dwell in your hearts through faith. And I pray that you, being rooted and established in love, may have power, together with all the Lord's holy people, to grasp how wide and long and high and deep is the love of Christ, and to know this love that surpasses knowledge—that you may be filled to the measure of all the fullness of God.

Now to him who is able to do immeasurably more than all we ask or imagine, according to his power that is at work within us, to him be glory in the church and in Christ Jesus throughout all generations, for ever and ever! Amen.

How does this address our FOMO?

Does this help to answer the previous question about being "rich toward God"? What does the richness of this relationship with God look like, feel like, act like? What clues do you find in this prayer?

Is there anything we can do to make this prayer come true, or is it entirely up to God? (We're not looking for a theological argument here, but how we can participate in this work of God.)

Do you think this surpassing love of Christ is something that we receive and enjoy or something that we share with others—or both? When a person is loved with this amazing love of Christ, how does he or she act toward others?

3. Read together Ruth 1:15-21:

> *"Look," said Naomi, "your sister-in-law is going back to her people and her gods. Go back with her."*
>
> *But Ruth replied, "Don't urge me to leave you or to turn back from you. Where you go I will go, and where you stay*

I will stay. Your people will be my people and your God my God. Where you die I will die, and there I will be buried. May the LORD deal with me, be it ever so severely, if even death separates you and me." When Naomi realized that Ruth was determined to go with her, she stopped urging her.

So the two women went on until they came to Bethlehem. When they arrived in Bethlehem, the whole town was stirred because of them, and the women exclaimed, "Can this be Naomi?"

"Don't call me Naomi," she told them. "Call me Mara, because the Almighty has made my life very bitter. I went away full, but the LORD has brought me back empty. Why call me Naomi? The LORD has afflicted me; the Almighty has brought misfortune upon me."

We got the backstory from the video. Ruth was from Moab, and she was leaving *her* home country to accompany her mother-in-law back to Bethlehem. Why would she do this?

How appreciative does Naomi seem to be?

Put yourself in Ruth's sandals. Your situation is just as bitter as Naomi's. You have lost your husband. You have no way to make a living. There is famine in the land. How can you possibly see an "open door" in this situation?

What are some opportunities that can arise from tragic circumstances? Have you ever experienced this?

4. Read together Ruth 2:8-12:

Boaz said to Ruth, "My daughter, listen to me. Don't go and glean in another field and don't go away from here. Stay here with the women who work for me. Watch the field where the men are harvesting, and follow along after the women. I have told the men not to lay a hand on you. And whenever you are thirsty, go and get a drink from the water jars the men have filled."

At this, she bowed down with her face to the ground. She asked him, "Why have I found such favor in your eyes that you notice me—a foreigner?"

Boaz replied, "I've been told all about what you have done for your mother-in-law since the death of your husband—how you left your father and mother and your homeland and came to live with a people you did not know before. May the LORD repay you for what you have done. May you be richly rewarded by the LORD, the God of Israel, under whose wings you have come to take refuge."

Remember that Boaz was the landowner, and Ruth was gleaning in his fields—picking up loose grain left by the reapers. Why does Boaz show such kindness to her?

Boaz prays that God would bless and reward Ruth, but then he also blesses and rewards her by offering support and protection. When we ask God to bless people, does that also involve a commitment on our part to do good to them?

When Ruth originally committed to stay with Naomi, do you think she imagined she would be rewarded like this? She eventually married Boaz. Do you think she imagined *that* blessing would come to her? Do you think she treated Naomi so well *because* she expected to be rewarded in the future?

5. Read together Galatians 6:2:

Carry each other's burdens, and in this way you will fulfill the law of Christ.

What "law of Christ" is this referring to? How does helping others "fulfill" that law?

What burdens are you aware of among the people you know? How can you help carry them?

IN CLOSING

John Ortberg said, "Open doors are everywhere, every day, and when we follow God's leading, we receive the blessing of seeing the world and our place in it as he sees it."

As you end this session today, let your mind's eye survey your world—your family, your church, your neighbors, your coworkers. There are people with burdens who need help carrying them. You have a part to play in their lives. In the silence now, pray for those people whom God brings to your mind, but also listen for what part God might be asking *you* to play.

Before session 5, complete the "On Your Own between Sessions" section. You might want to review that section at the beginning of session 5.

ON YOUR OWN BETWEEN SESSIONS

1. Besides Ruth's story, there are several other examples in the
   Bible of love "opening doors" for people. See how this played
   out in the lives of these people:

   Barnabas (Acts 4:36-37; 9:27; 11:19-26; 13:2-3)

   The widow of Zarephath (1 Kings 17:7-24)

   Abigail (1 Samuel 25)

2. This next activity might hurt a little. This self-analysis is not
   intended to make you feel guilty but to alert you to possible
   danger zones. In the earlier discussion of the Fear of Missing
   Out, we noted that our culture supports a craving for *more*—
   more stuff, more thrills, more energy. This is not always a
   bad thing, but it can distract us from a desire for a deeper
   relationship with God.

   On a scale of 0 to 10, how much power do the following things
   have in your life? On the chart below, gauge the power of your
   desire for more of these things. Circle the appropriate number
   on each line. Obviously, there's no scientific measurement here,
   just your self-analysis of which temptations are most powerful
   in your life.

   MORE APPROVAL FROM OTHERS/FAME/REPUTATION

   0 -------- 1 -------- 2 -------- 3 --------4 -------- 5 --------6 -------- 7 --------8 -------- 9 --------10

MORE EXCITEMENT/PASSION/THRILLS

0 -------- 1 ------- 2 -------- 3 --------4 -------- 5 --------6--------- 7 --------8-------- 9 --------10

MORE POSSESSIONS/LATEST TECH

0 -------- 1 -------- 2 -------- 3 --------4 -------- 5 --------6--------- 7 --------8-------- 9 --------10

MORE SECURITY/SAVINGS/INSURANCE

0 -------- 1 -------- 2 -------- 3 --------4 -------- 5 --------6--------- 7 --------8-------- 9 --------10

MORE COMFORT/PLEASURE/EASE

0 -------- 1 -------- 2 -------- 3 --------4 -------- 5 --------6--------- 7 --------8-------- 9 --------10

MORE DEPTH IN RELATIONSHIPS

0 -------- 1 -------- 2 -------- 3 --------4 -------- 5 --------6--------- 7 --------8-------- 9 --------10

MORE SATISFACTION/FULFILLMENT FROM SERVING OTHERS

0 -------- 1 -------- 2 -------- 3 --------4 -------- 5 --------6--------- 7 --------8-------- 9 --------10

MORE INTERACTION WITH GOD

0 -------- 1 -------- 2 -------- 3 --------4 -------- 5 --------6--------- 7 --------8-------- 9 --------10

As you look back over the chart, note those areas that compete with the last three entries. What can you do to be less like the rich fool of Luke 12:13-21 and more tuned in to the spirit of Paul's prayer in Ephesians 3:14-21?

3. Life Experiment: The Overlooked. In the video, John Ortberg said, "Doors open when we actually notice and care about people we might otherwise overlook."

   Pick a day this week to *notice* people you often overlook. The clerk, the receptionist, the mail carrier, etc. Take a moment to think about their lives: what needs, struggles, or joys might they have? If possible, pray silently for them when you see them—or assemble a list and pray through it later. For this exercise, there is no need to do a good deed for them, though a smile and a greeting might go a long way. And there's no telling what God might ask you to do.

4. Mission: Opening Doors. What can you do, using your unique knowledge and resources, to provide an opportunity for someone else? You might find inspiration from the story of Peter in the video, who served others by *employing* them, even if they were generally unemployable. He didn't just do a good deed for them; he gave them a chance to serve others in meaningful ways.

   So look around at your family, your church family, your friends, your neighbors. Is there someone who could use an opportunity—a job, a recommendation, an introduction, an internship, an investment, an idea, a challenge? How can you set an open door in front of someone else?

   Think about it, pray about it, and go for it.

5. Meditation: What If? What have you been complaining about lately? What have you been troubled by? Are there people or people groups in this world that your heart goes out to? Has God planted within you a desire to help?

Take some serious time to mull over this, to pray, to feel, to weep . . . and to dream. Let the Holy Spirit waft through your imagination. Ask, "What if?" What could happen if you and others, empowered by God, threw yourselves into a helping ministry? Turn off your negative filters for now. Imagine that anything is possible . . . because, you know, it is.

RECOMMENDED READING

In preparation for session 5, you may want to read chapter 8 of *All the Places to Go*.

THE JONAH COMPLEX

Sometimes open doors are not fun. Sometimes they're not even safe. Always they're about something greater than our own benefit. Often they lead to Nineveh. Nineveh is the place God calls you where you do not want to go. Nineveh is trouble. Nineveh is danger. Nineveh is fear. What do you do when God says to you, "Go to Nineveh; go to the place you do not want to go"? Because God will say that to you.

ALL THE PLACES TO GO, CHAPTER 8

VIDEO TEACHING NOTES

As you watch the video, use the space below to take notes. Some key points and quotes are provided here as reminders.

Josh's Story

Josh grew up with a passion for building things out of wood. But he ended up pursuing a more sensible career in teaching and then insurance, which left him unfulfilled. God led Josh into a career change, and he now builds furniture out of reclaimed wood.

QUOTABLE: "Work becomes worship when I see that I'm fulfilling what I'm supposed to be doing."

Teaching 1: John Ortberg

We often resist going through the doors God opens.

Jonah did exactly that.

> He was called to preach *against* Nineveh.
> Nineveh was powerful and cruel.
> Jonah went the opposite direction—to Tarshish.

We do that too. When God calls us to a daunting task, we often resist or run away.

QUOTABLE: "The antidote to fear is the presence of God. In him we are courageous."

While Jonah is on the boat, sailing away from God's door, God opens another door "in disguise." (Jonah is given an opportunity to connect with the Gentile sailors.)

QUOTABLE: "How many open doors are all around me—someone feels alone, someone waits to be inspired, someone is aching with rejection, someone is racked with guilt—just waiting for me to pay attention?"

Hardwin's Story

Since Hardwin is a physician, people often suggested that he go on medical mission trips, but he resisted. Eventually, he stepped out of his comfort zone and went.

Teaching 2: John Ortberg

Back to Jonah.

> On the boat, he recognizes his guilt and asks to be thrown overboard.
> The sailors don't do it at first, then they do, but . . .
> . . . this becomes a kind of worship service (they pray and "sacrifice").
> Jonah "hits bottom" and is swallowed by a fish; he prays.

QUOTABLE: "So often, we don't call out to God until we hit bottom."

> Jonah is vomited onto land.
> Jonah's story is a comedy. Joy wins.
> Between the lines, we see Christ.

The real reason for Jonah's resistance is a failure of love.

By contrast, when Jonah finally preaches in Nineveh, we see God's compassion, as he accepts their repentance and withholds judgment.

QUOTABLE: "Lack of love makes it easy for me
to say no to the door."

Jonah appreciates God's grace in creating a vine for shade, but not in redeeming a lost city.

VIDEO GROUP DISCUSSION

1. In the video, we met two skilled people at different points in their service to God. Which of them did you most identify with?

Josh was sort of lost careerwise, until the Lord brought him back to the woodworking he had always loved. Meanwhile, Hardwin knew exactly what his calling was as a cardiologist, but he felt there would be no place for that skill on a mission trip. Do you think churches in general have a narrow sense of what skills can be used in God's service?

If so, what can we do about that?

How has God used your special interests and skills to serve him?

Do you think God usually calls us to do the things we love to do, or does he challenge us to do things we don't feel comfortable doing?

2. Josh used an interesting phrase in his interview: "God started to download an idea on me." (In his case, the idea was to make a wooden table for his wife.) Is "download" a good description

of how God communicates with us, or would you say it some other way?

How do *you* begin to sense God's leading in a case like that—especially if it leads to a career change? Is it a voice, a sense, an idea, advice from a friend, or something else?

3. Have you ever found yourself in Jonah's situation, where God wanted you to do something and you resisted? If so, what happened?

John Ortberg mentioned a number of reasons for resistance—especially fear or lack of love, or perhaps a lack of imagination about what God can do. In your case, what caused the resistance?

4. When Jonah was on the boat, John Ortberg said there were other doors opening to Jonah, but they were "heavily disguised." What did he mean by that? How can a door of opportunity be disguised?

Has an opportunity come to you while you were resisting another one? What happened?

5. We talk about "hitting bottom" in certain circumstances of our lives. In Jonah's case, that was almost literal, as he was thrown into the sea and ended up in a fish's guts. What happens to people when they "hit bottom" in their lives? Do they, like Jonah, cry out to God, or do they keep resisting?

Have you ever had an experience like that?

GROUP BIBLE EXPLORATION

1. Read together Nahum 1:14-15:

> *The LORD has given a command concerning you, Nineveh:*
>> *"You will have no descendants to bear your name.*
> *I will destroy the images and idols*
>> *that are in the temple of your gods.*
> *I will prepare your grave,*
>> *for you are vile."*
>
> *Look, there on the mountains,*
>> *the feet of one who brings good news,*
>> *who proclaims peace!*
> *Celebrate your festivals, Judah,*
>> *and fulfill your vows.*
> *No more will the wicked invade you;*
>> *they will be completely destroyed.*

How long has it been since you studied the book of Nahum? This obscure minor prophet spoke out against Nineveh, which was the capital city of Assyria, the nation that had swept away the northern kingdom of Israel and was terrorizing the southern kingdom of Judah. What does the first part of this passage tell us about Nineveh?

To whom is the last part of this passage addressed? What is the message to them?

When God told Jonah to preach against this same city, Nineveh, what sort of message do you think Jonah expected to deliver—one of destruction and the grave or one of good news and peace?

2. Read together Jonah 1:12-16:

"Pick me up and throw me into the sea," [Jonah] replied, "and it will become calm. I know that it is my fault that this great storm has come upon you."

Instead, the men did their best to row back to land. But they could not, for the sea grew even wilder than before. Then they cried out to the LORD, "Please, LORD, do not let us die for taking this man's life. Do not hold us accountable for killing an innocent man, for you, LORD, have done as you pleased." Then they took Jonah and threw him overboard, and the raging sea grew calm. At this the men greatly feared the LORD, and they offered a sacrifice to the LORD and made vows to him.

In the video, John Ortberg said, "This pagan boat becomes a place of worship." Why did he say that? What worship do you see in this scene?

Do you think Jonah intended to inspire worship in these Gentile sailors?

Why do you think the Scriptures include this detail about the Gentile sailors? What does it tell us about God, humanity, and the prophet business?

Do you find that, as you go through your life as a Christian, you spread the Good News whether or not you intend to? In what ways does this happen in your life?

3. Read together Jonah 2:7-9:

When my life was ebbing away,
I remembered you, LORD,
and my prayer rose to you,
to your holy temple.
Those who cling to worthless idols
turn away from God's love for them.
But I, with shouts of grateful praise,
will sacrifice to you.

What I have vowed I will make good.
  I will say, "Salvation comes from the LORD."

This was the conclusion of Jonah's prayer from the belly of the fish. How would you describe Jonah's attitude at this point?

Who do you think he was talking about when he mentioned "those who cling to worthless idols"?

Based on these verses, what do you expect Jonah to preach to the Ninevites?

4. Read together Jonah 3:10–4:3:

When God saw what [the Ninevites] did and how they turned
from their evil ways, he relented and did not bring on them the
destruction he had threatened.
  But to Jonah this seemed very wrong, and he became angry.
He prayed to the LORD, "Isn't this what I said, LORD, when
I was still at home? That is what I tried to forestall by fleeing
to Tarshish. I knew that you are a gracious and compassionate

God, slow to anger and abounding in love, a God who relents from sending calamity. Now, LORD, take away my life, for it is better for me to die than to live."

Talk about a plot twist! There are two here. If you were reading this story for the first time, would it surprise you that Nineveh repented? Why or why not?

Why do you think Jonah responded as he did? Wasn't this a victory? Wasn't he asking them to repent?

Do you think Jonah's response here had anything to do with why he resisted in the first place?

5. Read together 1 John 4:18-19:

There is no fear in love. But perfect love drives out fear, because fear has to do with punishment. The one who fears is not made perfect in love. We love because he first loved us.

The word *perfect* in Scripture has the sense of "complete, fully grown." How does a "fully grown" love drive out fear?

We've been talking about resistance to the opportunities God gives us. Sometimes we resist because we're afraid. Was that Jonah's problem? How would "perfect love" change Jonah's approach?

If God asks you to do something scary for him, how do you handle that? Deny the fear? Gather your courage? Focus on your love for the task? Focus on God's love for you? Or all of the above?

IN CLOSING

As you end this session today, consider how God might be calling you. Have you been ignoring his call out of fear? Or out of a lack of love? Or is it a lack of imagination—assuming God couldn't possibly need you to, say, make wooden tables or provide cardiac care in the developing world? Take a moment in the silence to clear out the obstacles, to listen to God's voice, to envision that open door.

Before session 6, complete the "On Your Own between Sessions" section. You might want to review that section at the beginning of session 6.

ON YOUR OWN BETWEEN SESSIONS

1. Another Bible character who had some hesitations about doing what God asked was Gideon. Read his story in Judges 6–7.

   Why was he resisting?

   How did he try to determine what God wanted?

   What did he ultimately do? How did it turn out?

2. Self-analysis: Obstacles. On those occasions when you're acting like Jonah—resisting what God is asking you to do—what is the cause of your resistance?

To make this very visual, use this circle to create a pie chart. How big a slice of your resistance is due to each of the following factors?

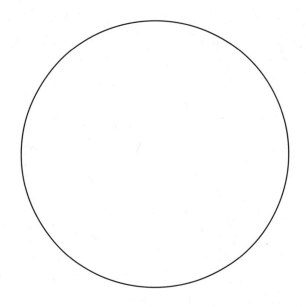

- fear
- lack of love
- insecurity about your own ability
- assumptions about what can (and can't) be done
- not paying attention
- being distracted by other activities
- other (name your own)

As you look at your completed chart, what can you do to tackle your main obstacle? How can you become more responsive to God?

3. Jonah's story is full of interesting twists and turns. Could you use your artistic skills to create something based on that story? A picture (or graphic novel). A song (maybe based on that second chapter). A playlist. A poem. A dance. A play. A sculpture. A tapestry. Maybe even a wooden table. You don't have to cover the whole story, but find some moment in it, some attitude, some theme, and bring it to life.

4. Life Experiment: To-Do List. Is there something you *should* do that you've been putting off? Almost everybody has some sort of "to-do list" with items that linger there for a while. Can you find a particular task that's more than just a common chore—something you're pretty sure God would like you to do? Contacting an old friend. Helping out in some ministry. Or just fulfilling a promise to your spouse. It doesn't need to be a major spiritual issue, but something that would make God happy if you got it done.

Pick a day this week to do it. Ask God for the strength of will to accomplish it. Seek his wisdom in doing it right. Pay attention to the obstacles that, even now, crop up. Pray about those as well. And then, just do it.

We're not talking about any major rebellion here, but still . . . you've turned a long-term *no* into a *yes*. How does that feel?

5. Confession: Take some time to quiet down before God. Remove the distractions as best you can. Turn off your phone. Put yourself in a private place. If it helps to focus on a Bible passage, try Jonah 2. Then talk with God about those places he wants you to go—and about whatever resistance you've been putting up. Confess any bad attitudes you've been harboring, and commit yourself to follow his leading.

    Listen for his forgiveness, his reassurance, his wisdom, and his continuing direction.

RECOMMENDED READING

In preparation for session 6, you may want to read chapters 9–10 of *All the Places to Go*.

THANK GOD FOR CLOSED DOORS

I don't know why some prayers get yeses and some prayers get nos. I know the anguish of a no when you want a yes more than anything in the world. But I don't know why. I only know that in the Cross God's no to his only Son was turned into God's yes to every human being who ever lived. . . . Doors close because God has plans I don't know.

ALL THE PLACES TO GO, CHAPTER 9

VIDEO TEACHING NOTES

As you watch the video, use the space below to take notes. Some key points and quotes are provided here as reminders.

Charlie's Story

Charlie lost his home and his job as a youth pastor after a difficult divorce. His life was "deconstructed." Through this crisis, he came to see God in a new, more intimate light.

QUOTABLE: "My healing began when I first started to face the pain."

Teaching 1: John Ortberg

Jesus knew about unanswered prayer from Gethsemane.

QUOTABLE: "At the heart of the gospel is an unanswered prayer. . . .
Because the ultimate answer to every human anguish, including
the anguish of unanswered prayer, is the Cross, where Jesus Christ,
the Son of God himself, suffered."

Jesus told his disciples they would feel grief when he left them,
but later joy would come.

We have questions, just as the disciples did. Jesus answers with "in a
little while" things will be set right.

Todd's Story

Successful in business, Todd was suddenly demoted. He worked
through that disappointment by starting a charity to combat AIDS
in Africa.

Teaching 2: John Ortberg

What might God be up to behind closed doors?

We may be knocking on the wrong door.

The ultimate door is the doorway to heaven. (The veil in the Temple was opened.)

Jesus is the door.

QUOTABLE: "Jesus became an outsider so we could be invited in."

Why don't we run through doors with reckless abandon?

> Are we overwhelmed by our own inadequacy?
> But God will help us.
> We should "forget what is behind" (our inadequacy).
>
> Do we doubt God's goodness?
> Don't forget the price he has paid for us.
>
> Are we too afraid?
> But what we need is not what's behind the door.
> We need the one who goes with us: the Lord.

VIDEO GROUP DISCUSSION

1. In this session's video, we met a couple of people who went through major crises—loss of job, loss of marriage, and loss of home. You may know people who are going through problems like these, where their hopes and dreams have been shattered. What can you say to them?

   Do you think it's even harder to face such crises when people feel that it was God's will for them to have that job or that marriage? Is there an extra level of loss when they have to rethink God's will for their lives? What can you say in a case like that?

2. In the first interview, Charlie said something very interesting: "God was teaching me how to hold things with open hands, how to not force things or control things." What do you think he meant by that?

How could such an open-handed approach help you deal with a personal crisis?

3. In this video, John Ortberg made a rather astonishing comment: "At the heart of the gospel is an unanswered prayer." What was he talking about?

How does that idea help us deal with situations in which God doesn't give us what we've prayed for?

4. Jesus' disciples were always asking questions, and we're full of questions too. More than anything, we want to know why there is such suffering in human life. John Ortberg zeroed in on Jesus' comment that "in a little while" they would feel grief (when he left them) and "in a little while" their grief would turn to joy (when the Holy Spirit came upon them). How can this "in a little while" concept help us deal with life's suffering?

5. In all this talk about open doors, John Ortberg reminded us that Jesus *is* the door. Does that mean it really doesn't matter what we do with our lives as long as we're Christians? Why or why not?

GROUP BIBLE EXPLORATION

1. Read together Luke 22:39-44:

   Jesus went out as usual to the Mount of Olives, and his disciples followed him. On reaching the place, he said to them, "Pray that you will not fall into temptation." He withdrew about a stone's throw beyond them, knelt down and prayed, "Father, if you are willing, take this cup from me; yet not my will, but yours be done." An angel from heaven appeared to him and strengthened him. And being in anguish, he prayed more earnestly, and his sweat was like drops of blood falling to the ground.

   How would you describe the emotional state of Jesus at this point?

   What was Jesus praying for?

How did his Father respond?

What did the angel do? Why do you think God sent the angel?

Have you ever prayed for something that didn't happen? How does this story affect your attitude toward that unmet longing?

2. Read together John 16:19-22:

Jesus saw that they wanted to ask him about this, so he said to them, "Are you asking one another what I meant when I said, 'In a little while you will see me no more, and then after a little while you will see me'? Very truly I tell you, you will weep and mourn while the world rejoices. You will grieve, but your grief will turn to joy. A woman giving birth to a child has pain because her time has come; but when her baby is born she forgets the anguish because of her joy that a child is born into the world. So with you: Now is your time of grief, but I will see you again and you will rejoice, and no one will take away your joy."

What was Jesus talking about in this passage?

If you were in that room, and if you had the opportunity to ask one more question, what would you ask?

How long is "a little while"? Is Jesus talking about minutes, months, or millennia?

Why does Jesus draw a comparison to a woman giving birth? How does that image help us deal with our own struggles?

The psalmists and prophets often asked, "How long, O LORD, how long?" (See Psalm 13:1-2; 82:2; Habakkuk 1:2.) They were complaining about injustice in the world and the hard circumstances faced by believers. How does Jesus address that question in this passage?

3. Read together 2 Corinthians 12:7-9:

In order to keep me from becoming conceited, I was given a thorn in my flesh, a messenger of Satan, to torment me. Three times I pleaded with the Lord to take it away from me. But he said to me, "My grace is sufficient for you, for my power is made perfect in weakness."

Scholars disagree on this, but do you have any guesses about what Paul's "thorn in the flesh" was?

Whatever it was, how do these verses describe the problem?

Do you think Paul was wrong to ask God to take it away? Why or why not?

How did the Lord respond to this request?

In what ways is the Lord's grace "sufficient" in situations like this?

How is his power "made perfect" in our weakness?

How does this passage affect your outlook on those times when the Lord doesn't give what you ask for?

4. Read together Philippians 3:10-14:

I want to know Christ—yes, to know the power of his resurrection and participation in his sufferings, becoming like him in his death, and so, somehow, attaining to the resurrection from the dead.

Not that I have already obtained all this, or have already arrived at my goal, but I press on to take hold of that for which Christ Jesus took hold of me. Brothers and sisters, I do not consider myself yet to have taken hold of it. But one thing I do: Forgetting what is behind and straining toward what is ahead, I press on toward the goal to win the prize for which God has called me heavenward in Christ Jesus.

How can we "know Christ"? Do we know him even better when we "participate in his sufferings"?

Finish this sentence: "I want to know Jesus. In Gethsemane, Jesus experienced a closed door. Therefore, when I experience a closed door . . ."

There is some great wordplay in this passage. Paul uses the same verb—"take hold of"—in four different ways. (It's translated "obtained" once.) Work that out. Who has taken hold of—or will take hold of—what, or whom?

In our continuing discussion of closed doors and open doors, how can the final sentence of this passage help us? What do we "forget" and what do we "press on toward"?

5. Read together Psalms 24:7-8:

Lift up your heads, you gates;
  be lifted up, you ancient doors,
    that the King of glory may come in.
Who is this King of glory?
  The LORD strong and mighty,
    the LORD mighty in battle.

This psalm starts by declaring God's ownership of the whole earth, but it quickly navigates to Jerusalem. That's where the "gates" and "ancient doors" are. Picture this in your mind. What scene is this passage describing?

In poetry, images can have multiple meanings. Those gates and ancient doors of Jerusalem can refer to other entryways, too. As you think about this series on open doors, what possible interpretations can you come up with for these verses?

As you dare to walk through the open doors God sets before you, why is it important that the Lord is "strong and mighty"?

IN CLOSING

This is the last session of the *All the Places to Go* study, but don't let these challenges drift away. God has set open doors before you, and he has slammed other doors shut. Through it all, he walks with you. The King of Glory opens doors as he goes. Are you walking with him and getting to know him better on the journey?

In these closing minutes, talk with God about the doors in your life. Thank him for the closed doors, and ask for wisdom and courage to go through the doors he throws open in the future.

In the next few days, you might want to try some of the "On Your Own" exercises on the following pages.

ON YOUR OWN IN THE COMING DAYS

1. Bible Study: Joseph. How can we deal with doors that close? It would be hard to find a better guide to answer this question than Joseph. Read his story in Genesis 37 and 39–46. Trace how he dealt with each setback and how the Lord opened new doors for him along the way.

2. Self-analysis: Doors Opened and Closed. Grab a few sheets of paper. Map out a time line of your life, including childhood. Include three to eight major events in your life.

Then, below the line, at the appropriate points, include the doors that closed: the school you didn't get into, the job you didn't get, etc.

Above the line, add the open doors—opportunities that came your way. At the top of the page, put the doors you actually "walked through." (These might duplicate some of the major events on the time line.)

So your pages should look something like this:

(The Xs are specific events/opportunities in your life, which you can label.)

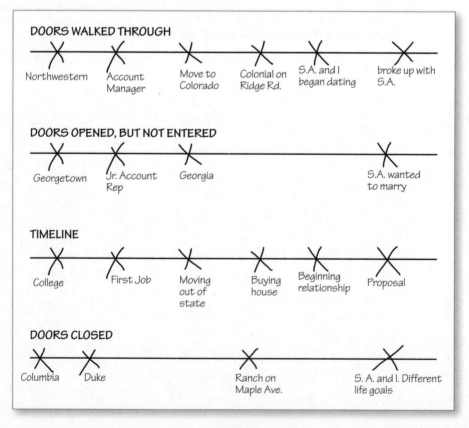

DOORS WALKED THROUGH

| Northwestern | Account Manager | Move to Colorado | Colonial on Ridge Rd. | S.A. and I began dating | broke up with S.A. |

DOORS OPENED, BUT NOT ENTERED

| Georgetown | Jr. Account Rep | Georgia | | | S.A. wanted to marry |

TIMELINE

| College | First Job | Moving out of state | Buying house | Beginning relationship | Proposal |

DOORS CLOSED

| Columbia | Duke | | Ranch on Maple Ave. | | S. A. and I. Different life goals |

As you look back over your time line, what do you see? Don't focus on regrets about unentered doors, but learn from them. How did the closed doors open *you* up for what God would do with you later?

3. Art Project: Door. Adapt this to your own artistic preferences, but here are some ideas that revolve around the door theme.

   - Write a play, video script, story, or poem about a person going through a door.
   - Take photos of various doorways. Create a slide show or collage.
   - In your best calligraphy, pen a few Bible verses about doors. Hang them up or snap photos of your handiwork and post them online.
   - Find a doorway in your home that you can decorate in a way that commemorates the "doors" God has set before you and your family. This could be a point of instruction for your children or a continuing reminder for yourself.

4. Meditation: Thank God for Closed Doors. Set yourself in front of a closed door, and look at it. Then think back through the closed doors in your life—rejections that might have been painful at the time, heartfelt prayers that weren't answered the way you wanted, etc. Talk with God about them and, even more important, *listen* to what he says. Can you come to a place of peace about these things? Can you thank him for the closed doors in your life?

5. Life Experiment: Open Door Group. Can you gather a group of friends who will meet regularly (perhaps once a month) *for the purpose of discussing open doors God is setting before each of*

you? Make sure this group sets a policy of encouragement. No unnecessary slamming of doors here. Let God lead each of you into uncharted territory. Imagine adventurous ministries that will use your unique gifts and stretch you further. How can your group pool your collective gifts and resources to take advantage of new opportunities?

About the Author

JOHN ORTBERG is an author, speaker, and the senior pastor of Menlo Park Presbyterian Church (MPPC) in the San Francisco Bay Area. His books include *Soul Keeping*; *If You Want to Walk on Water, You've Got to Get Out of the Boat*; *The Life You've Always Wanted*; *The Me I Want to Be*; and *Who Is This Man?* John teaches around the world at conferences and churches.

Born and raised in Rockford, Illinois, John graduated from Wheaton College and holds a master of divinity and doctorate degree in clinical psychology from Fuller Seminary. Prior to joining MPPC, John served as teaching pastor at Chicago's Willow Creek Community Church. John is a member of the Board of Trustees at Fuller Seminary, serves on the board for the Dallas Willard Center for Spiritual Formation, and is a former board member of Christianity Today International.

Now that their children are grown, John and his wife, Nancy, enjoy surfing the Pacific to help care for their souls. He can be followed on Twitter @johnortberg.